CLASSIC ROCK BANDS

LED ZEPPELIN

by Laura K. Murray

CONTENT CONSULTANT
Jack Hamilton
Assistant Professor
Media Studies and American Studies
University of Virginia

An Imprint of Abdo Publishing | abdobooks.com

abdobooks.com

Published by Abdo Publishing, a division of ABDO, PO Box 398166, Minneapolis, Minnesota 55439.

Printed in China.
052021
092021

Cover Photo: Michael Ochs Archives/Getty Images
Interior Photos: David Redfern/Redferns/Getty Images, 4–5, 8; Jay Thompson/Globe Photos/Zuma Press, Inc./Alamy, 11; Pictorial Press Ltd/Alamy, 14–15, 24–25, 62; Jorgen Angel/Redferns/Getty Images, 19, 22; Charles Bonnay/The LIFE Images Collection/Getty Images, 28, 40, 96; dpa/picture-alliance/dpa/AP Images, 31; AP Images, 32–33; Robert Knight Archive/Redferns/Getty Images, 36–37; Digital Reflections/Shutterstock Images, 45; Michael Ochs Archives/Getty Images, 46–47; Daily Record Mirrorpix/Newscom, 52; PF1/WENN/Newscom, 54–55, 78–79; Bruce Alan Bennett/Shutterstock Images, 58–59, 65; Terence Spencer/The LIFE Images Collection/Getty Images, 68–69; Michael Putland/Hulton Archive/Getty Images, 74–75; Veronica Farley/AP Images, 82; Amy Sancetta/AP Images, 86; Kevin Mazur/Getty Images Entertainment/Getty Images, 88–89; Richard Drew/AP Images, 93

Editor: Melissa York
Series Designer: Colleen McLaren

Library of Congress Control Number: 2019954381

Publisher's Cataloging-in-Publication Data

Names: Murray, Laura K., author.
Title: Led Zeppelin / by Laura K. Murray
Description: Minneapolis, Minnesota : Abdo Publishing, 2022 | Series: Classic rock bands | Includes online resources and index.
Identifiers: ISBN 9781532192005 (lib. bdg.) | ISBN 9781532179907 (ebook)
Subjects: LCSH: Led Zeppelin (Musical group)--Juvenile literature. | Rock and roll bands--Biography--Juvenile literature. | Rock musicians--Great Britain--Biography--Juvenile literature. | Psychedelic rock music--Juvenile literature.
Classification: DDC 782.42166--dc23

CONTENTS

CHAPTER ONE

Rocking the Garden

On July 29, 1973, nearly 25,000 people packed into the indoor arena at Madison Square Garden in New York City. They swarmed to see the four-member British rock band Led Zeppelin, whose newest album was at the top of the charts. The performance marked the end of the band's sold-out, three-night stint at the Garden. It was also the final show of the band's grueling ninth North American tour.

About ten songs into a set list that included a mix of new and already-classic tracks such as "Black Dog," "Over the Hills and Far Away," and "Whole Lotta Love," the stage went dark. "I think this is a song of

By the time of the band's 1973 performances at Madison Square Garden, Led Zeppelin was a band on top of the world.

hope," announced lead singer Robert Plant as the band began "Stairway to Heaven."[1]

The bluish light washing over the darkened stage created an atmosphere that transported the audience. Guitarist Jimmy Page, dressed in a black jumpsuit emblazoned with a glittering dragon, plucked out broken chords on a double-neck electric guitar. Bandmate John Paul "Jonesy" Jones played on his keyboard, producing a lilting, recorder-like sound. Plant commanded the microphone bare-chested in skintight jeans, a spotlight illuminating his long, wavy blond hair.

As the song progressed, Plant's voice grew louder and he threw his hair back. Mustached drummer John "Bonzo" Bonham entered with a pounding beat as the tempo increased. About six minutes in, Page took over with a blistering, three-minute guitar

"Stairway" Legacy

In 1973, Led Zeppelin's tour de force track "Stairway to Heaven" was already a well-known rock song. It had been released two years earlier on the band's untitled fourth album, which has been praised by some music critics as the greatest heavy metal album of all time and has sold nearly 40 million copies. "Stairway to Heaven" grew in popularity through Zeppelin's enthralling live performances and remains one of the band's best-known songs decades after its release, although Plant later stopped singing it, saying he could no longer relate to the song.

solo under the blazing colored lights, his fingers flying over the frets. Supported by Bonzo's drums, Jones's keyboard, and Plant's dancing tambourine, he whipped the crowd into a frenzy. The song ended with Plant's a cappella warble, "And she's buying a stairway to heaven," before he unleashed a final, wailing note over the worshipful crowd.

> "I think I'm just learning how to play the guitar. Sometimes when I'm on stage, I only get a flash of what my potential really is."[3]
>
> – *Jimmy Page, 1973*

STAIRWAY TO STARDOM

By its 1973 tour, Led Zeppelin mania was in full swing, with US newspapers comparing the band's effect on fans to that of the Beatles nearly a decade earlier. Throughout the tour, Led Zeppelin broke attendance records across the country, bringing in more than $4 million total.[2]

One of the secrets to Led Zeppelin's success was their multitalented foursome. Each member was a standout musician and performer. After working individually in the music industry, they found nearly immediate success in 1968 as a group first known as the New Yardbirds. Soon they changed their name to Led Zeppelin and catapulted to fame, combining

A double-neck guitar was one of the weapons in Page's impressive arsenal.

their talents to produce ever-evolving rock music like the world had never heard.

First, there was Plant, the strutting front man with soaring vocals, creative lyrics, and attitude to spare. Then there was Jones, the quiet innovator who was as impressive a bassist as he was a keyboardist, organist, and sound mixer. Next, there was Bonham, who awed crowds and fellow musicians alike with his drum strokes that could be at turns riotous or groovy. Finally, there was Page, whose otherworldly guitar skills included sometimes wielding a violin bow across his guitar strings, to the delight of audiences. Each of Zeppelin's four members would become a rock and roll legend in his own right.

> "What Bonzo could do on the bass drum with a single foot pedal was just outrageous."[4]
>
> *– Bev Bevan, drummer for rock band Electric Light Orchestra*

ALL THAT GLITTERS

Led Zeppelin's new brand of rock music came on the heels of the counterculture movement that had introduced the likes of the Beatles, the Rolling Stones, Bob Dylan, and Janis Joplin. Led Zeppelin was something else entirely. Strange lyrics, gripping riffs, crashing drums, howling vocals, sauntering attitudes, and grand performances made for a combustible combination, bewitching audiences and dividing critics. The members of Led Zeppelin infused their songs with varying influences

Lengthy Songs

Led Zeppelin's tracks often ran longer than the usual three-to-four-minute singles by other artists. The band's longest song recorded was "In My Time of Dying" off its sixth album, *Physical Graffiti*, released in 1975. It clocked in at 11 minutes and six seconds. Playing live, Zeppelin was known for improvisational sets in which songs could stretch to 40 minutes and include lengthy solos showcasing the members' musical skills. By 1977, the live solos were longer than ever, with Bonham's frenzied drum solo on "Moby Dick" and Jones's keyboard solo on "No Quarter" each stretching to 30 minutes or more.

The offstage lives of Led Zeppelin have become a signature part of the band's legend and legacy.

from folk, blues, funk, and psychedelia, mixing in experimental sounds and fantasy lyrics. Their songs sometimes lasted three times as long as contemporary singles played on the radio, and they went on even longer when played live.

Through the years, the band became more than their music—it personified a wild lifestyle that oozed the burgeoning rock and roll themes of fame, money, and excess. As their popularity skyrocketed, Led Zeppelin's music sometimes was overshadowed by the band members' controversial behavior that veered into danger and eventually ended in tragedy. Criticisms of the band have continued today, often regarding perceived misogynistic attitudes and lyrics. The group has also been plagued by legal issues over copyrights and accusations of plagiarism. One of the most prevailing rumors even accuses them of worshipping the devil. Surrounded by myth and legend, Zeppelin's legions

Ranking Zeppelin Songs

In 2019, *Rolling Stone* contributors created a list ranking what they viewed as the 40 best Led Zeppelin songs. The top five included:

5. "Ramble On" (1969)
4. "Kashmir" (1975)
3. "Black Dog" (1971)
2. "Stairway to Heaven" (1971)
1. "Whole Lotta Love" (1969)

Other media outlets, including *Vulture*, *Ultimate Classic Rock*, and *Spin*, have released their own lists with varying favorites.

122 DEAL 830
10 GIANT SIZE
RINSO
WITH
COLOR BLEACH
10¢ OFF

Led Zeppelin Members

Led Zeppelin was a versatile foursome of musicians. On drums was John "Bonzo" Bonham (born 1948), who built his first drum set out of kitchen containers at age five. Bonham's own skills were mostly self-taught. He left school as a teenager to play music and work construction. On bass and keyboard was John Paul Jones (born John Baldwin in 1946), who played piano from a young age and listened to big band, blues, and jazz music. During his music studies, he began playing bass. He joined his first band at age 15. On guitar was Jimmy Page (born 1944), who began playing the instrument at age 12 and was mostly self-taught. He was drawn to rock and blues music, counting guitarists of the early rock and roll style of rockabilly music among his influences. Page left school at age 15 to pursue music. Finally, on vocals was Robert Plant (born 1948), who was influenced by early rock and blues, leaving home at age 16 to pursue his musical interests. His keen interest in mythology and history found its way into much of Zeppelin's music.

of fans have found it difficult to separate fact from fiction. The most famous biography about them, 1985's *Hammer of the Gods* by Stephen Davis, outlined many of the most notorious stories. However, the band members contest its accuracy.

Led Zeppelin is considered one of the greatest rock bands of all time. They are credited with giving rise to rock genres from metal to punk to alternative and steering the evolution of rock music. Although often categorized as pioneers of heavy metal, the band members historically dismissed that label. Whatever their genre, Led Zeppelin continues to inspire contemporary musical artists while attracting new fans of all ages and remaining one of the best-selling musical acts ever. To date, the band has sold an estimated 300 million albums worldwide, with reissued albums climbing the charts decades after their initial release.[5]

At Madison Square Garden in 1973, Led Zeppelin's fame was entering its peak. They were the biggest and, to hear some fans and music journalists tell it, best band in the world. They felt like rock gods and were treated as such. But time would tell whether the rock and roll lifestyle would take its toll or whether the luster of fame was everything it appeared to be.

CHAPTER TWO

On the Wings of Yardbirds

Led Zeppelin's roots can be traced to another British band, the Yardbirds. Formed in 1963, the Yardbirds were a blues-based rock band that found mainstream success once they began producing songs with a more commercially popular sound. That change in musical direction didn't sit well with the Yardbirds' lead guitarist, blues purist Eric Clapton, who opposed what he viewed as sacrificing quality for popularity. On the same day the Yardbirds' first major hit, "For Your Love," was released in March 1965, Clapton announced his departure from

Page, *left*, began his musical career as part of the Yardbirds.

the band. He did, however, have a recommendation for his replacement—a young guitarist named Jimmy Page.

Just 21, Page was already a well-known guitarist who was making a living as a session musician. Page initially declined the Yardbirds job, possibly because he didn't want to risk his steady income by touring with the group. Page suggested his friend Jeff Beck for the position, who accepted.

As it turned out, Page did join the Yardbirds in 1966, initially as a temporary fill-in bassist. He stayed on, touring as lead guitarist when Beck fell ill. He eventually became half of a lead guitar team with Beck. When Beck left the band in late 1966, Page continued as the Yardbirds' solo lead guitarist. Meanwhile, he had his sights set on other ventures.

Yardbirds Legacy

A storied band in its own right, the Yardbirds boasted a trio of legendary guitarists passing through its ranks: Eric Clapton, Jeff Beck, and Jimmy Page. Clapton went on to a successful career with the band Cream and as a solo artist. Beck received acclaim as a solo artist, while Page founded Led Zeppelin. The Yardbirds were inducted into the Rock & Roll Hall of Fame in 1992, credited for their innovations in sound that shaped psychedelic rock, progressive rock, and punk. The Yardbirds' pioneering techniques included using sound distortion and feedback within their recordings. The group got back together in 2003. Jim McCarty remains the Yardbirds' only original member.

GETTING THE BAND TOGETHER

Earlier that year, Page joined Beck, bassist John Paul Jones, drummer Keith Moon of the Who, and pianist Nicky Hopkins to record a song called "Beck's Bolero." The experience got Page thinking about forming a rock supergroup made up of already successful musicians. Initially, Page suggested forming a group that included Moon, Beck, Jones, and the Who's John Entwistle, but Moon reportedly joked that the idea would go over "like a lead zeppelin," meaning it would work as well as an airship made out of metal.[1] Still, Page kept thinking about his idea during the next two years.

Meanwhile, the Yardbirds' commercial success began to fizzle even as the members

"Beck's Bolero"

Recorded in 1966 and released the following year as the B side of Jeff Beck's first single, "Hi Ho Silver Lining," the rock instrumental "Beck's Bolero" was based on French composer Maurice Ravel's orchestral piece *Boléro*. The recording had been secretive, with the Who's disgruntled drummer, Keith Moon, sneaking into the London studio disguised in a hat and sunglasses. The song has since cemented a place for itself in rock and roll lore, being considered one of the best rock tracks of all time and influencing the likes of Jimi Hendrix, Duane Allman, and other famous guitarists. Although Page was credited as the song's writer and Mickie Most as its producer, controversy has continued through the years over what role everyone played.

By 1967 Page was employing experimental new techniques, such as using a violin bow to play his guitar.

continued touring, recording, and experimenting with new sounds. It became increasingly clear that the bandmates had differing visions about the type of music the Yardbirds should produce. By mid-1968, the Yardbirds' diverging interests led to the departure of vocalist Keith Relf and drummer Jim McCarty for their own projects, leaving Page and guitarist/bassist Chris Dreja as the remaining members. Former professional wrestler and actor Peter Grant managed the band.

Page was undeterred by the breakup, seeing it as an opportunity to pursue his idea of a supergroup. Despite others' skepticism, 24-year-old Page had a clear artistic vision for what he wanted to do, and he already had enough professional experience to be confident he could deliver.

Once Dreja decided to leave the Yardbirds to pursue photography, Page was left to assemble the lineup, with Grant still by his side. First, he secured Jones, a masterful, classically trained keyboardist, bass player, and arranger with a penchant for experimental music. For a vocalist, Page approached Terry Reid, who was a well-known support act for bands such as the Rolling Stones and Cream. Reid declined, but he recommended 18-year-old blues singer Robert Plant.

Although Plant was relatively inexperienced, the teenager's singing chops impressed Page, whose

OMRYSTES

Making Magic

Page and Jones came to Led Zeppelin as experienced professional musicians. Besides his time with the Yardbirds, Page had played on hit songs for artists such as Burt Bacharach, the Kinks, and Van Morrison. Jones had begun touring with musicians at age 17 and had since played or arranged for acts including Cat Stevens, Dusty Springfield, Shirley Bassey, the Rolling Stones, and Rod Stewart. On the other hand, Plant and Bonham didn't have the same industry or recording experience. When the four got together, however, the chemistry was undeniable.

decision was confirmed when further meetings revealed their similar musical tastes. Plant also helped lock the group's final piece into place when he recommended his friend and former bandmate John "Bonzo" Bonham as the new group's drummer. Bonham, who worked as a carpenter between drumming gigs, had extraordinary power, technique, and above all, volume. Although reluctant at first, Bonham took the job. Page's vision of a rock supergroup was on its way to becoming a reality.

"THIS WAS GONNA WORK"

There was one issue: the Yardbirds still had tour dates left to fulfill in Scandinavia. Page's new group had to learn to play together, and fast, but the guitarist wasn't worried. "I was absolutely convinced that all that was needed was for us all to get in a room," he later said. "'Cause I knew that the material I had was really good. It's nothing that they'd ever really played before. . . . It was only a matter, really, of getting it together. I knew this was gonna work."[2]

Page's confidence proved to be well founded. In August 1968, the four musicians met in a London basement for their first rehearsal. To kick things off, they played a popular Yardbirds tune, "Train Kept A-Rolling." The song was originally recorded by American musician Tiny Bradshaw in 1951 and received the rock treatment by Johnny Burnette and the Rock 'n Roll Trio in 1956. When Bonham, Jones, Page, and Plant took their turn at the song, they were amazed at the energy in the room. Afterward, everyone started laughing. "Maybe it was relief, or maybe from knowledge we could groove together," Page remembered. "And that was it."[3]

Just a few weeks later, the group played its first gig at a teen club in Denmark on September 7, 1968. They called themselves the New Yardbirds. "Jimmy Page has put a new band together," announced one press review. "The music

"There is no doubt that [Plant] is a good singer, but he doesn't have to twist his body like he's having a ruptured appendix, does he?"[4]

– Press review of the New Yardbirds

The first performance of the New Yardbirds set the stage for the birth of Led Zeppelin.

is the same, only better than ever."[5] During the end of the eight-day tour through Scandinavia, the group continued to gel. They also learned that they would legally need to find a new name. Their manager, Grant, suggested co-opting Keith Moon's reference to a lead zeppelin as the band's moniker. The bandmates approved, and Grant suggested dropping the *a* in *lead* to prevent Americans from pronouncing it as *leed*. Led Zeppelin was born, and rock music would never be the same.

What's in a Name?

The story of Led Zeppelin's name has varied over the decades, but the version in which Keith Moon joked about a rock supergroup involving him going over like a lead zeppelin is the generally accepted version. Page later asked Moon for his blessing to use the name. Others involved assert that it was the Who's bassist, John Entwistle, who responded to Moon's comment of a "lead balloon" by saying, "More like a lead zeppelin."[6] Page later stated, "The name wasn't really as important as whether or not the music was going to be accepted. . . . We could have called ourselves the Vegetables or the Potatoes, but I was quite keen on Led Zeppelin."[7]

CHAPTER THREE

Lead Balloon Rising

In the fall of 1968, the members of Led Zeppelin arrived at London's Olympic Studios to begin recording their debut album. The band had been playing together for a matter of weeks, but the process went unusually quickly, helped along by the group's collective excitement and the studio experience of Page and Jones. After just nine days and a total of 30 hours in the studio, the nine-track album was complete. As producer and self-appointed creative director, Page footed the bill to see his vision come to life, as the group did not yet have a recording contract.

With the band's lineup solidified, it was time for Led Zeppelin to create their first album.

The album would be released early the next year. Meanwhile, Grant was busy lining up gigs. The group made its official debut as Led Zeppelin on October 25, 1968, at England's Surrey University. Grant continued booking the group at increasingly larger venues throughout England, but when the British media didn't pay much attention, he turned his sights to the United States. The move was later considered by biographers and music journalists to be a deciding factor in Zeppelin's lasting success.

> "[Peter] Grant changed attitudes within the music industry, so that attention was focused on the needs of the artists, often at the expense of the record companies, tour promoters, and agents—who didn't always appreciate his methods."[1]
>
> *– Journalist Chris Welch*

Led Zeppelin made their US debut on December 26, 1968, at the Denver Auditorium Arena in Colorado, opening for American band Vanilla Fudge. Zeppelin played through the initial nerves of stepping on stage and soon felt the audience's receptive energy. They played more than 20 minutes over their allotted time, sending Vanilla Fudge members reeling at the prospect of following the act. The crowd loved Page's slicing guitar, Plant's keening vocals, Bonham's powerhouse drums, and Jones's rhythmic grooves. While critical reviews were lukewarm, the Denver crowd—and successive American audiences—had no such reservations.

> "Jimmy Page revolutionized everything. There was no real blues rock in that bombastic way before Zeppelin. Plus, with the insane drumming of John Bonham, it was radical, playing at a very, very high level—improvisational on a big-rock scale. It was brand new."[2]
>
> *– Producer Rick Rubin*

EXPLOSIVE PERFORMANCES

At the time of their American debut, Led Zeppelin was unknown—newly formed and without an album or even a track playing on the radio. This relative anonymity turned out to be liberating for the bandmates, easing the pressure of having to live up to expectations and leaving the band free to perform as creatively as it wanted. Crowds were floored by the supercharged, no-holds-barred musical stylings of the group. They wanted more, and Led Zeppelin was eager to deliver.

Soon audiences across the continent had heard of Led Zeppelin, with the band quickly building a base of fervent fans as it worked through North American tour stops into early 1969. Since Zeppelin had only nine songs on their yet-unreleased album,

The band quickly became known for its high-energy performances, and its fan base steadily grew.

they played covers to fill in their sets. The band often used a well-known song as a base around which to improvise for several drawn-out minutes, with each band member adding his own elements and solos to make the song the band's own.

The group members overpowered the acts they were opening for—so much so that headlining bands either refused to go on after them or didn't show up at all. Zeppelin had no problem filling more time. In Boston, Massachusetts, the band reportedly performed for four hours at the insistence of the crowd, playing its entire set and adding improvised covers of Elvis Presley, the Beatles, and any other material it could work out.

"With no hits of their own to speak of as yet, the idea was simply to lift an audience previously oblivious to their music as high and as fast as possible, leaving them utterly drained and spent by the end, giving whoever followed the band onto the stage an almost impossible task. And it worked."[3]

– *Biographer Mick Wall,* When Giants Walked the Earth

INTRODUCING ZEP TO THE WORLD

Led Zeppelin's self-titled debut album was released in January 1969 through Atlantic Records, an iconic American R&B label that had been looking to expand further into the rock market after its success with such bands as Cream, Iron Butterfly, and Vanilla Fudge. Grant negotiated Zeppelin a five-year contract worth a reported $220,000 that included an advance payment of more than $140,000 for the first year.[4] According to biographer Mick Wall, the tremendous sum was the largest advance ever offered to a new artist with no established fan base. Grant also secured Led Zeppelin unprecedented control over their albums, tours, and promotion.

A Rocking Tea Party

On January 26, 1969, Led Zeppelin performed the last of four shows at the Boston Tea Party concert venue in Massachusetts, playing for hours in front of an ecstatic crowd that wouldn't let them off the stage. Steven Tyler, later known as the front man of Aerosmith, reported being at the legendary show and being overcome with emotion during "Dazed and Confused." For Zeppelin, it was the night that foreshadowed the massive success and rapturous reception the band would have. "I suppose it was then that we realized just what Led Zeppelin was going to become," Jones remembered.[5]

Featuring black-and-white cover artwork of the infamous 1937 explosion of the airship *Hindenburg*, the *Led Zeppelin* album found enormous sales success. Atlantic Records promoted it heavily, and radio stations put it into their regular rotation. The album eventually reached Number 6 on the UK charts. The songs showed a variety of styles, including

Led Zeppelin's innovative approaches in the studio and live on stage demonstrated the promise of the young band.

psychedelic blues and heavy rock, with folk and classical elements thrown in. Combined, it was a gut punch of intensity.

Led Zeppelin's first album cover memorably depicts the destruction of the airship *Hindenburg*.

Of the album's nine tracks, three were original, including "Good Times Bad Times," "Communication Breakdown," and "Your Time Is

Gonna Come." The rest of the tracks were based on or borrowed from the work of other artists, including "Black Mountain Side" and "Dazed and

Confused." While some musicians felt that all music was fair game to use, the fact that Zeppelin often did not credit or acknowledge the original creators—and withheld the subsequent financial rewards—would result in heavy criticism for decades to come.

Hindenburg Disaster

Led Zeppelin's debut album cover depicted an exploding zeppelin—an image of the famous *Hindenburg* disaster. On May 6, 1937, the German passenger airship LZ 129 *Hindenburg* caught fire while landing in New Jersey, killing 36 people. Later in Led Zeppelin's career, a descendant of the von Zeppelin family that manufactured the *Hindenburg* tried to stop the band from playing in Denmark, seeing its use of the Zeppelin name and the image of the disaster as disrespectful. To avoid legal action and continue with their scheduled Copenhagen show, Zeppelin played under the name "The Nobs."

Several music critics panned the album, beginning a long-standing animosity between Zeppelin and certain media outlets. *Rolling Stone* magazine famously described the album as "dull," "weak," and "much-overdone," criticizing the group's focus on Page.[6] Other reviewers, however, credited the album for its explosive energy as well as Zeppelin's innovative techniques, which included backward echo—playing a recorded echo backward—and creatively rearranging microphones and amplifiers. They also moved Bonham out of the traditional drummer's booth to play in the same area as the band during recording. These techniques were signs of a band with the imagination to try new things instead of being content to produce the sounds of the past. It was an exciting prospect for fans who couldn't wait to hear what the group would create next.

Musical Hindsight

Many present-day music critics credit Led Zeppelin's debut album as a revolutionary force, citing its skill, intensity, production, and sound effects. It was particularly impressive from a foursome who had begun playing together just a few weeks earlier. Almost as memorable were the negative critiques of what would become such an influential rock album. More than 30 years after *Rolling Stone* panned Zeppelin's debut album, the magazine gave an updated review, this time rating the album five out of five stars. "There may be better, more refined Zep albums . . . but none sounds quite as gratifyingly raw or is as comprehensive in defining the band's intentions," wrote Greg Kot in 2001.[7] However, the original reviewer, John Mendelsohn, stood by his initial negative impression.

CHAPTER FOUR

The Time Is Now

Led Zeppelin capitalized on their fans' energy by embarking on an exhausting series of tours, including a second North American circuit that began in April 1969. This time around, critics paid more attention to the contributions of the bandmates other than Page. However, many music writers remained critical of the band, commonly labeling it "overhyped," a criticism that continued to upset the band members, who had reportedly memorized their *Rolling Stone* album review "word for word."[1] Even as some critics grumbled about Zeppelin's loud volume, long hair, and startling intensity,

Plant, Jones, and Page arrived at a 1969 tour stop in Hawaii carrying the in-progress tapes for *Led Zeppelin II*.

PAN AM

young fans flocked to the electrifying new group.

> "You didn't have to be a genius to know Zeppelin was going to be a smash. . . . People were going crazy!"[2]
>
> *– Promoter Barry Frey on Led Zeppelin's first US show*

There was no doubt that Grant's decision to bring Led Zeppelin to the United States was paying dividends as the band started another US tour in late 1969 following its first full UK tour. Led Zeppelin would play six US tours in addition to international stops in 1970, breaking attendance records as they packed in hordes of enthusiastic fans. Already the band was building a wild lifestyle as success began to materialize in the form of money, fans, and status.

Cover Faces

Artist David Juniper created the album cover for *Led Zeppelin II*, basing it on a World War I (1914–1918) photo of the German air force that included the famous fighter pilot nicknamed the Red Baron. Juniper edited the photo to add the faces of Led Zeppelin, along with the band's manager Peter Grant and tour manager Richard Cole. Among the faces is actress Glynis John, who was reportedly featured as a nod to the similarly named recording engineer Glyn Johns.

LED ZEPPELIN II

Zeppelin's second album, *Led Zeppelin II*, was released in October 1969 to more than 400,000 advance orders and generally positive reviews. A notable exception was *Rolling Stone*, which slapped the band with another scathing review. This criticism helped to intensify the band members' resentment of the magazine. The album sold three million copies within six months, and it held the top spot on the *Billboard* chart for seven weeks, overtaking the Beatles' classic album *Abbey Road*.[3] The album featured a heavy rock sound that the band would expand in future releases. Three of the nine tracks on *Led Zeppelin II* were based on blues songs, while the other six were originals. It was the first album to include Plant as a songwriter. Tracks included "Ramble On," written by Page and Plant. The song, which included references to J. R. R. Tolkien's classic fantasy series The Lord of the Rings, was a study in contrasts, combining loud and soft as well as acoustic and electric elements.

Led Zeppelin II also demonstrated the band's developing identity and musical chemistry. In its 2012 list of "500 Greatest Albums of All Time," *Rolling Stone* ranked *Led Zeppelin II* at number 79, attributing the album's power to the combination of "[Page's] white-blues devilry, John

"[T]hey made one of the greatest, heaviest, and raunchiest albums ever, steeped in both Delta and Chicago blues, '60s psychedelia, and gentle-to-bone-crushing dynamics."[4]

– Music journalist Patrick Doyle on Led Zeppelin II

The recording sessions for *Led Zeppelin II* took place in mid-1969.

Bonham's hands-of-God drumming, Robert Plant's misty-mountain howl, and John Paul Jones's firm bass and keyboard colors."[5]

WHOLE LOTTA PROBLEMS

To Zeppelin's chagrin, Atlantic Records released one of the tracks, "Whole Lotta Love," as a single. As a principle, the band was against releasing songs as singles—it wanted people to buy the entire album. Page later recalled that the group hated what it saw as the "abbreviated, canned format" of singles, remarking, "I wanted to develop our songs emotionally."[6] He explained that the band created the album so that it was an "uneditable expression" that needed to be aired as a single work.[7] Of course, a full album cost more than a single, making album sales much more profitable.

Throughout Led Zeppelin's active years, several singles were released in the United States and other countries, although none came out in the United

Whole Lotta Love

Page wrote the famous guitar riff for "Whole Lotta Love" on his houseboat in England. To produce the psychedelic guitar sound, Page detuned his guitar—a Sunburst Les Paul Standard he bought from soon-to-be Eagles guitarist Joe Walsh—and pulled the strings. A faint echo of Plant's voice on the track was an accident to which Page and mix engineer Eddie Kramer added reverb to make it sound intentional. The song reached Number 4 on the *Billboard* chart and would remain Led Zeppelin's only top-10 single in the United States. It has been lauded as a revolutionary rock song, with journalist Cameron Crowe commenting, "It's not a song, it's a siege."[8] In 2007, "Whole Lotta Love" was inducted into the Grammy Hall of Fame.

Kingdom. In the case of "Whole Lotta Love," the label also cut the song down from 5:33 to 3:12 for radio play. Listeners loved the track, which featured an iconic riff by Page on his Les Paul guitar. By April 1970, the song was certified gold by selling one million copies. Page said he heard the edited-down version once and, repulsed, never listened to it again.

> "Page's riff was Page's riff. It was there before anything else. . . . At the time, there was a lot of conversation about what to do. It was decided that it was so far away in time and influence that . . . well, you only get caught when you're successful. That's the game."[9]
>
> *– Robert Plant on the "Whole Lotta Love" lawsuit, 1990*

"Whole Lotta Love" also ignited controversy, as its lyrics were taken from "You Need Love," a 1962 song recorded by American blues singer Muddy Waters and written by Willie Dixon. Another British band, Small Faces, had also recorded a version of the song in 1966. Dixon, who was not credited on Led Zeppelin's initial release, sued Zeppelin in a case that was settled out of court in 1987. Dixon's credit was added to later releases of the album.

A NEW DIRECTION

In 1970, Led Zeppelin embarked on their largest US tour yet, including their first shows at New York's Madison Square Garden. In October, the band released its third album, *Led Zeppelin III*, which offered a more experimental sound than the first two albums and incorporated more folk- and acoustic-styled songs, mixing the sounds of heavy rock ("Immigrant Song") with folk-inspired music ("That's the Way"). Jones's use of synthesizer and string arrangements helped shape the new sound. Page and Plant had written much of the album at a secluded cottage in Wales, known as Bron-Yr-Aur, where Plant had spent parts of his childhood.

Inspiration from Iceland

Plant wrote the lyrics to "Immigrant Song" after Led Zeppelin played a 1970 concert in Reykjavik, Iceland, in the month of June—the time of year in the country in which the sun does not fully set. Aligning with Plant's interest in fantasy and legend, this song, the wailing opening track of *Led Zeppelin III*, alludes to Norse mythology and is told from a Viking chieftain's point of view.

Led Zeppelin III would become the group's most divisive album among critics, many of whom panned what they saw as the band's abrupt shift in direction. Some accused the band of jumping on board with the acoustic sound that was gaining

> "I was doing a long drum solo every night on tour and my hands were covered in blisters."[11]
>
> *– John Bonham on the 1970 tours*

in popularity at the time with bands such as Crosby, Stills & Nash. That accusation particularly rankled Page, who pointed out that Zeppelin's first albums also had acoustic tracks. According to sound engineer Terry Manning, Page correctly predicted before the album's release, "This is so different, this is going to shock people."[10] Page and the band seemed to recognize that in order to make a lasting impression on the music world, they had to resist efforts to box themselves into one particular sound or genre.

The group's third album also sparked a long-running rumor that Led Zeppelin members, and particularly Page, were involved in black magic and devil worship. This stemmed from Page's idea to have phrases inscribed into the groove of the vinyl

Deals with the Devil?

Page was enthralled with the life and works of occultist Aleister Crowley, later purchasing Crowley's home on Loch Ness in Scotland. Page also bought an occult bookshop that dealt with tarot, astrology, and other subjects, as well as the supposedly haunted Tower House in England. Page didn't dispel the rumors regarding his involvement with the occult, which continued to grow in magnitude along with Led Zeppelin's popularity.

Led Zeppelin III was musically more diverse than the band's previous albums.

album: "So Mote Be It" on one side and "Do What Thou Wilt" on the other. Both are attributed to British occultist and writer Aleister Crowley (1875–1947). This connection to the occult only served to intensify the speculation and mystique surrounding the band.

CHAPTER FIVE

Climbing to New Heights

In 1971, Led Zeppelin's fame was growing quickly, but the process wasn't always smooth. When the band decided to play at smaller venues to better connect with the fans, the plan backfired. Thousands of people without tickets tried to get into the small venues, spurring fights and other unrest. These incidents added to the band's feeling that it couldn't shake negative public perception. Another tour began that spring, but it was marred by a violent riot July 5 in Milan, Italy. The set descended into chaos as inciters clashed with police, who shot tear gas into the crowd. Fires, violence, and

The simple, iconic cover of Led Zeppelin's untitled fourth album featured rustic wallpaper and a framed photo of a hunched man carrying branches.

injuries followed in what music journalists later described as a "war" scene.[1]

On November 8, 1971, Led Zeppelin released their fourth album. When the album shot to the top of the charts, the record industry had an interesting conundrum—it was unclear what to write in the charts since the album didn't have a name. Its cover had only the image of a bearded man carrying a pack of sticks on his back. Sometimes known as *Led Zeppelin IV*, the album was commercially labeled "Untitled" or "Four Symbols," referring to the four markings on the inner sleeve and label that symbolized the band members. Page had the idea to keep the album unnamed in response to the critics who continued to slam the band for

Unrest in Belfast

In March 1971, Led Zeppelin played the first stop of their small-venue tour at Ulster Hall in Belfast, Northern Ireland. The city was in turbulence at the time, with Catholics and Protestants involved in a long-standing violent political conflict about Northern Ireland's independence. Near the concert hall, demonstrators set fires in the streets. Inside, however, Led Zeppelin and their crowd were focused on the music. "The young people of the town, unconcerned with ancient conflicts, used their energy to celebrate the worthwhile cause of peace, love, and music," reported Chris Welch in *Melody Maker* magazine.[2] The concert was the first public performance of songs from Zeppelin's upcoming fourth album, including "Black Dog," "Going to California," "Rock and Roll," and "Stairway to Heaven."

being overhyped. According to Page, it was about the music, not the name.

Four Symbols

On Led Zeppelin's untitled fourth album, each band member chose a symbol to represent him. Plant chose a feather inside a circle, based on symbols from a mythical ancient civilization. Bonham selected three intertwined rings. Jones chose three interlocking leaf shapes within a circle, which resembled a Celtic knot. Page designed his own symbol—a sign that looks like letters spelling out "ZoSo"—whose meaning he has never revealed. Theories posed by Zeppelin enthusiasts have ranged from astrological connections to the secret of the universe. Page once revealed the meaning to Plant, who has since said he's forgotten what Page told him.

The band had laid down the tracks at a mobile recording station that belonged to the Rolling Stones as well as at the Headley Grange studio space in England. The result would become their best-selling album. It included the heavy rock song "Black Dog," with its memorable riff by Jones—based on a Muddy Waters song—as well as an acoustic track based on Scottish folklore called "The Battle of Evermore." Sandy Denny, a female singer from the folk group Fairport Convention, contributed vocals to the track. The folk-inspired "Going to California" featured Page on acoustic guitar and Jones on mandolin. It was rumored to be about singer-songwriter Joni Mitchell, of whom Page and Plant were avid fans. "When the Levee Breaks" was an electric blues and rock combination reworked from a 1927 song by Kansas Joe and Memphis Minnie, who were credited on later releases. "Rock and Roll" featured pianist Ian Stewart of the Rolling Stones. The album also included the rock ballad "Stairway to Heaven," which didn't garner much notice until the band began playing it live, leaving audiences mesmerized. The song went on to become Led Zeppelin's most famous track, as well as one of the most famous rock songs of all time. Some sources claim it to be the most requested and most played song on rock radio.

Headley Grange

Built in 1795 in Hampshire County, in England, Headley Grange originally served as a workhouse and was later converted to a recording and rehearsal space. The house offered a spooky atmosphere and rich acoustics, showcased in one instance when Led Zeppelin's sound engineer Andy Johns set up Bonham in a stairwell to record the drums on "When the Levee Breaks." Several other songs on Zeppelin's fourth album were written at Headley, including Plant's lyrics to "Stairway to Heaven" and the title for "Black Dog," which referenced a black Labrador that prowled the grounds. Still, not everyone was content to sleep in the old mansion—Plant and Bonham reportedly refused to stay there overnight and headed to a hotel instead.

HOUSES OF THE HOLY

By 1973, Led Zeppelin's star had risen even higher as the band worked on its follow-up album. On March 26, they released their fifth album, *Houses of the*

Holy. The album included tracks such as "Over the Hills and Far Away," "The Song Remains the Same," "The Ocean," "The Rain Song," and "No Quarter." The reaction to the latest album was mixed among fans and critics, with a reviewer in *Rolling Stone* labeling the band "Limp Blimp."[3] Others, however, saw the album as a creative masterpiece, with its incorporation of styles such as reggae, blues, and classical propelling rock music forward in a way that detractors did not understand.

Mixed critical reactions didn't stop the band from pulling in gigantic crowds. In May 1973, their ninth North American tour began with a record-breaking performance in Atlanta, Georgia. The estimated attendance of 49,233 shattered the stadium's previous attendance record, held by the Beatles, by more than 16,000.[4] At the May 5 show in Tampa, Florida, the band attracted a crowd of more than 56,000, the largest audience for a single performance in the United States. This time, the record unseated the historic 1965

"To put it bluntly, there is simply no way that one can relate the frenzied mediocrity of Grand Funk, Black Sabbath, and Deep Purple with the class and calibre of Led Zeppelin. . . . The price of pop success may be enormously high . . . but Led Zeppelin is one band with the stamina to handle it."[5]

– Journalist Ritchie Yorke, 1973

ZEPPELIN

The band shot to new heights of fame as the 1970s continued.

Beatles performance at New York's Shea Stadium. "You get to a point where you enjoy playing so much you don't want to come off stage," Jones said.[6]

The feeling was mutual, with the majority of concertgoers stunned by the artistry and chemistry between the bandmates. "What makes Zeppelin so overpowering is that all four are superb musicians," wrote music journalist Clint Roswell, adding that the live shows showcased sounds different from those in the recordings. "They are all so keenly aware of the integral flow of the music that each responds precisely and creatively to the other."[7] The band's concert sets never had the same sound twice, with the members continually improvising and playing off each other in what Page called "a mysterious adventure every night."[8]

Backward Messages

A lasting rumor about Led Zeppelin's connection to dark forces originated in the early 1980s from radio preacher Michael Mills, who claimed that Plant's vocals in "Stairway to Heaven" played backward revealed satanic messages. Led Zeppelin was not the first or last band accused of using the technique of backmasking—recording a sound backward—to hide controversial messages. The band's label said any similarities in sound were a coincidence, responding in a statement, "Our turntables only play in one direction—forwards."[9]

Led Zeppelin with the *Starship*, their private jet

SUPERSTAR STATUS

By the end of Led Zeppelin's 1973 tour, the millionaire bandmates were full-fledged rock stars who built a reputation for a high-rolling lifestyle of high-end treatment and out-of-control parties.

They even traveled by a private jet, known as the *Starship*, with the band's name written on it. Their concerts had grown in spectacle and performance, with the addition of light shows, smoke, mirrors, live doves, and increasingly flamboyant outfits.

Their music stylings grew more complex, with Jones playing organ, synthesized piano, and mellotron—a keyboard instrument that used prerecorded tapes inside. Page brought in a theremin, an electronic instrument controlled by hand movements made in the air. Meanwhile, Bonham used his drumstick to light the frame of a gigantic gong on fire. Plant, on the other hand, wielded his octave-climbing voice like an instrument in itself. Some critics denounced the showmanship as gimmicky, but fans were captivated.

The band members' offstage activities were beginning to inspire as many headlines as their performances. Their superstar status carried with it not only legions of fans and squadrons of limousines but also dangerous drugs, violent altercations, and death threats.

The partying and fast-paced lifestyle began to take a toll on the band. As Plant later said, "The kind of speed we were moving at, the creative juices in the air,

All Aboard

The *Starship* was a veritable flying party. Originally, pop singer Bobby Sherman and his manager bought the Boeing 720 from United Airlines and refurbished it to offer style and comfort. The outfitted jet that included an electric organ, video system, and fireplace became a status symbol of rock stars. After Led Zeppelin, other musicians to charter the *Starship* included Alice Cooper, Elton John, Peter Frampton, and the Rolling Stones.

the whole thing was just an absolute mixture of adrenaline, chemical, euphoria . . . and there were no brakes. We couldn't stop what was happening. We had no idea what it even *was*. But we just kept trying, pushing forward, every show."[10] By the end of 1973, Jones considered leaving the band to spend more time with his family and other music projects. He was known as the most practical, shy member of the group, generally content to stay away from the spotlight. Ultimately, band manager Grant helped convince Jones to stay, and Led Zeppelin continued their breakneck pace.

"Once I had all the time in the world and no money. Now I have the money but no time."[11]

– John Paul Jones

CHAPTER SIX

On Top of the World

In May 1974, Led Zeppelin started their own record label, Swan Song Records, under Atlantic Records. The label soon signed other rock artists, including Bad Company, Maggie Bell, and the Pretty Things. Meanwhile, the label's logo of a naked winged figure rising skyward became a recognized symbol of Led Zeppelin.

Never losing sight of their own music, the bandmates returned to Headley Grange and Olympic Studios to record new tracks. In February 1975, the band released the double album *Physical Graffiti* on Swan Song Records. Besides such new tracks as "Kashmir," "Ten Years Gone," and

The band played in huge venues in front of thousands of fans as its fame reached its apex in the mid-1970s.

"In My Time of Dying," the sixth album introduced a handful of previously unreleased songs from the band's recording sessions going back to 1970, including "The Rover" and "Black Country Woman."

Once again, the album showcased the many styles the band loved to incorporate, ranging from hard rock and blues to funk and folk. In particular, "Kashmir" was noted as an album standout. With lyrics based on a drive Plant took through the Moroccan desert, its distinctive Indian and Arabic influences, progressive rock flavor, and intricate section shifts combined for an epic track. The album marked a turning point of sorts in critical reception, as it was met with largely positive comments by previously skeptical reviewers.

Mysterious Figure

The Swan Song logo was based on an 1870 painting titled *Evening (The Fall of Day)*. The painting, by American artist William Rimmer, depicted the Greek god Apollo. The logo spurred much speculation surrounding whom or what the figure represented. A common suggestion was that it was the fallen angel Lucifer, a theory supported by Page's work on the soundtrack for the short film *Lucifer Rising*. At one point, Plant said the figure was Icarus, the figure in Greek mythology who flew too close to the sun. Some fans maintained that the blond-haired figure represented Plant with his signature wild mane.

FAME AND FORTUNE

The year 1975 was considered the peak for Led Zeppelin, with the group perceived by many as untouchable rock gods basking in wealth and fame. The band continued touring to sold-out crowds, with its combined album and tour revenue from its latest US tour estimated at more than $40 million, which is more than $185 million in today's dollars.[1] In March, each of Led Zeppelin's six albums was in the *Billboard* Top 200 chart simultaneously, with the recently released *Physical Graffiti* in the Number 1 spot.

> "I wish we were remembered for 'Kashmir' more than 'Stairway to Heaven.' It's so right—there's nothing overblown, no vocal hysterics. Perfect Zeppelin."[2]
>
> *– Robert Plant, 1990*

Their star status remained sky high, with Page and Plant featured on the cover of *Rolling Stone* with a cover story by teenage writer Cameron Crowe. The band saw the piece as a vindication of sorts from the magazine that had panned its debut album years before. Even the White House chimed in on Led Zeppelin, as US president

> "The key to Zeppelin's longevity has been change. . . . Album-wise, it usually takes a year for people to catch up with what we're doing."[3]
>
> *– Jimmy Page, 1975*

Page's skillful guitar solos thrilled fans at concerts around the world.

Gerald Ford's daughter, Susan, cited the group as her favorite band. Her brother Steven also reported playing "Stairway to Heaven" on the White House roof. "It's good to know they've got taste," Plant told *Rolling Stone*.[4]

Led Zeppelin shows now boasted video screens, laser lights, explosions, and fog machines. Not everyone was a fan, with *LA Times* critic Robert Hilburn describing one Zeppelin concert as "a numbing combination of intense, tenacious music and hopelessly limited imagination."[5] The band played without openers or a break, performing for several hours each show. "Myself, I get fed up with hearing about groups who only do a 50-minute show. It's not right," Page told Crowe

Teenage Journalist

Led Zeppelin's 1975 *Rolling Stone* cover story was written by 18-year-old rock enthusiast and Zeppelin fan Cameron Crowe, who was making a name for himself as the youngest contributor in the magazine's history. Since the magazine had so viciously panned Zeppelin's previous albums, Page in particular needed convincing to grant the interview. But Crowe had earned the band's trust after traveling with Zeppelin as he wrote a *Los Angeles Times* story. Encouraged by the Eagles' Joe Walsh, Page agreed to Crowe's *Rolling Stone* story and gave an insightful interview. Crowe went on to become a renowned screenwriter and director. His 2000 film *Almost Famous* was based on his time as a teenage writer on the road with bands such as Led Zeppelin. The song "Tangerine" from Zeppelin's third album is featured at the film's conclusion. *Almost Famous* won the 2001 Academy Award for Best Original Screenplay.

in *Rolling Stone*. "It all depends on how much a performer has got to say, I suppose, and Zeppelin has got quite a bit to put across."[6]

Swan Song Success

Led Zeppelin's Swan Song Records, active from 1974 until 1983, differentiated itself from other musical artists' so-called "vanity labels"—record labels dismissed as existing purely to feed the artists' egos. Instead, Swan Song found real success with several artists it signed. One of Swan Song's most successful acts was the rock group Bad Company, composed of Paul Rodgers and Simon Kirke (both formerly of the band Free), Boz Burrell of King Crimson, and Mick Ralphs of Mott the Hoople. Led Zeppelin's manager, Peter Grant, also managed Bad Company. The group's self-titled debut album reached the top of the charts. Another Swan Song group, the Pretty Things, had a Number 1 album with 1974's *Silk Torpedo*.

CRACKS IN THE FOUNDATION

Despite the success, the band was tiring of life on the road. Through true events, disputed retellings, and increasingly wild rumors, Led Zeppelin's growing reputation for general mayhem, self-indulgence, and excess spanned the globe. Stories involved riding motorcycles through hallways, fishing for sharks out hotel windows, trashing property, and increasing substance abuse. Armed guards escorted the band everywhere. Its large entourage included known gangsters who were typically armed and ready for a fight. Drugs

Bonham's behavior was particularly worrying to his fellow band members.

such as cocaine were a constant presence, and by the mid-1970s, Page and Bonham had begun using heroin.

Increasingly troubling was the behavior of Bonham, who was said to be particularly affected by life away from home and family. Friendly and approachable when sober, the drummer gained the nickname "The Beast" because he turned belligerent and violent while intoxicated. Bonham destroyed dressing rooms and hotel suites and was apt to throw punches and toss furniture off balconies. Once he punched a woman who smiled at him in recognition. By 1975, Bonham was becoming increasingly volatile as his drinking and drug use intensified. Journalists were warned to not make eye contact with him for their own safety.

Following Zeppelin's 1975 tour, the band members became tax exiles, leaving the United Kingdom to avoid paying the majority of their earnings as taxes to the British government. They would not be able to return to the United Kingdom until 1976. That meant months away from home with no touring in the country. While Bonham was upset at having to spend even more time away, Page and Plant

Macho Moves

Throughout the years, people have discussed Led Zeppelin's portrayal of men, women, and gender roles. Even the band's own fans have pointed out sexist or misogynistic undertones in the group's lyrics. Much has also been made of Zeppelin's cultivated macho image and use of stereotypical, aggressive masculinity as a part of heavy rock. Other bands in this camp include the Rolling Stones, the Who, and, later, Mötley Crüe and Poison. The criticisms are supported by some of the Zeppelin musicians' and crew members' offstage treatment of women and underage girls.

saw an opportunity to travel the world and play international shows.

However, events did not go as expected. In August 1975, the Plant family and Page's daughter Scarlet were traveling in Greece when their vehicle veered off a cliff and hit a tree. Scarlet's mother, Charlotte Martin, was following in the car behind and called for help. Plant suffered broken bones. His wife, Maureen, nearly died from a skull fracture. The Plants' two children were also hurt, though Scarlet was uninjured. With doctors cautioning that Plant might never walk again unaided, the upcoming Led Zeppelin tour was canceled.

CHAPTER SEVEN

Crashing Down

With the band's future uncertain and Plant still recovering from his injuries, Plant and Page headed to California to write new material with a sense of urgency and determination. After recording in Munich, Germany, Led Zeppelin released their seventh album, *Presence*, in April 1976 under their Swan Song label. The real-life drama of the car accident and the rawness of the band's current state came through in the completed tracks, which included the ten-minute "Achilles Last Stand" as well as "For Your Life."

Presence shot to Number 1 but didn't have the staying power of some of Zeppelin's

Plant spent time recovering with his family after the car accident.

previous albums. Reception was mixed even among the band members. Page and Plant were pleased with it, with the former later calling it "our best in terms of uninterrupted emotion," and the latter describing it as "a cry of survival."[1] Jones, on the other hand, felt more neutral toward the album, as he and Bonham hadn't had much input in its creation. Page had largely taken over the project as he had in the band's early days.

By then, Plant was able to walk unaided, although the band wasn't ready to begin live gigs yet. Meanwhile, the band released a concert film, *The Song Remains the Same*, which consoled fans who were hungry to see Zeppelin perform again. Despite the recent setbacks, Zeppelin hoped the next year

Led Zeppelin on Film

Led Zeppelin's much-delayed concert film, *The Song Remains the Same*, was released in 1976. It included footage from the band's 1973 performances at Madison Square Garden, along with scenes later reshot on a recreated stage. The retakes required Jones to wear a wig to match his longer hairstyle from the initial filming. The concert film produced a successful soundtrack and was part of a genre that included the Beatles' *A Hard Day's Night* (1964), the Rolling Stones' *Gimme Shelter* (1970), and the Band's *The Last Waltz* (1978). These types of rock documentaries were later parodied in the 1984 film *This Is Spinal Tap*, which followed a fictional British rock band and mocked stereotypical, over-the-top rock band behavior. Led Zeppelin was one of the filmmakers' direct inspirations.

would be their best yet. That, however, would not be the case.

1977 TOUR

After an absence of more than two years from the stage, Zeppelin began their long-awaited eleventh US tour on April 1, 1977, in Dallas, Texas. It had been delayed a little over a month as Plant recovered from laryngitis.

The band was set to travel to the 51-show tour on its latest mode of transportation—a private 45-seat Boeing 707 jet named *Caesar's Chariot*. More than 1.3 million tickets had sold at an astonishing rate, and the band again shattered attendance records at the first stops. "Zeppelin Soars to New Heights," read one newspaper headline following a California show.[2] One of their set pieces included a large model of Stonehenge, the mysterious prehistoric monument in Wiltshire, England. Fans were as fervent as ever, though some spectators began to complain that the band members' extended

> "Emerging like a gust of fresh air from the conceits and vanities of the flower-power era, Led Zep were a revelation—gutsy, honest, soulful, terrifyingly engaged, and, for all the visual overkill, masterfully in control of their material."[3]
>
> *– Music journalist William Langley, 2007*

solos—up to nearly 40 minutes in some cases—were getting extreme.

Despite the commercial success, things were slowly crumbling behind the scenes. An increasingly thin Page was in poor health, Plant was still in pain, and Bonham was more combustible than ever. Relations were increasingly strained as the band seemed caught up in its celebrity status and detached from the real world, reveling in privilege and suffering no apparent consequences for behavior such as property destruction, infidelity, and substance abuse. According to music journalist Lisa Robinson, doctors came on the road with the band to fill drug prescriptions, and heroin became an "unspoken fact of life around the band, management, and crew."[4] Meanwhile, riots broke out at some shows when fans who did not have tickets demanded entry. Events turned especially ugly backstage at a July concert in Oakland, California. Managers Grant and Cole, along with Bonham and band enforcer John Bindon, were involved in the brutal beating of a venue staff member. The incident ended with a SWAT team arresting the four at the band's hotel. They were later charged with assault. The case was settled out of court.

Days later, Maureen Plant called her husband from England. Their five-year-old son, Karac, had died suddenly of a respiratory infection. Plant, along with Bonham and a few others from the management team, rushed home. For unknown reasons, Page and Jones did not attend Karac's funeral. The tour was canceled.

> "We made our own laws. If you didn't want to . . . abide by them, don't get involved."[6]
>
> *– Tour manager Richard Cole*

During what Plant called "the darkest times of my life," he had to take a break from the band. The tragedy forced the singer to take stock of Led Zeppelin's rock and roll lifestyle and growing detachment to reality, later recalling: "The 1977 tour ended because I lost my boy, but it had also ended before it ended, really. It was just a mess. Where was the actual axis of all this stuff? Who do I go to if it's really bad for me? There was nobody. Everybody was insular, developing their own worlds."[5]

Riot in Tampa

After just a few songs on June 3, 1977, in Tampa, Florida, Led Zeppelin ended the show early due to a sudden storm. Rioting broke out among the disgruntled 70,000-plus fans, and police arrived with tear gas and clubs to remove people from the venue. The clashes resulted in dozens of injuries and more than 20 arrests.[7]

Jones sometimes played a triple-necked mandolin at concerts.

HOLDING IT TOGETHER

By late 1978, Zeppelin had slowly regrouped and begun recording their next album. Plant and Jones took a leadership role, allegedly due to Bonham's

alcohol addiction and Page's heroin addiction. According to Jones, "There were two distinct camps by then, and we were in the relatively clean one."[8]

In August 1979, Led Zeppelin released their eighth studio album, *In Through the Out Door*, through the Swan Song label. Recorded at Polar Studios in Stockholm, Sweden, the album's best-known tracks included "All My Love," written by Jones and Plant and dedicated to Plant's son, and "Fool in the Rain," which featured a samba breakdown from Bonham and was released as a successful single in the United States. Zeppelin's experimentation was on full display on tracks such as the ten-minute "Carouselambra," which highlighted work by Page on double-neck guitar and Jones on synthesizer. The album was a huge seller, reaching the top of the US, UK, Canadian, and New Zealand charts.

Purdie Shuffle

When John Bonham pounded out his iconic drum section on Led Zeppelin's "Fool in the Rain," he used a variation of a grooving drum pattern known as the Purdie Shuffle, created by American drummer Bernard Purdie. Purdie was known for his work in the R&B, soul, and funk genres. Throughout his career, Purdie played with acts including Aretha Franklin, Bob Marley, and Steely Dan.

By this time, punk music had emerged on the scene, with bands such as Sex Pistols and the Clash leading the way. Music journalist Lisa Robinson later recalled some members of the press depicting Led Zeppelin as "bloated, self-regarding dinosaurs" as compared with the punk rockers—ignoring Zeppelin's legacy as rock pioneers.[9] Others saw the recent album as another exciting departure that set up a new creative direction for the band. The bandmates were feeling optimistic about what lay ahead. What no one knew was that everything was about to collapse.

Knebworth Festival

Led Zeppelin's two shows at England's Knebworth Festival in August 1979 held special significance, as it was the first time the band had performed live together in the two years since Plant's son had died. The group had not performed in the United Kingdom for four years, so new and old fans alike were thrilled to see their idols live, and the press billed the gig as a comeback of sorts. The crowds each night were estimated to include more than 200,000 people, and they cheered on the band for multiple encores.[10] It would be the last time Led Zeppelin played together in their home country.

CHAPTER EIGHT

End of a Dream

Any hopes of future success were dashed by another devastating loss for the band—this time, one of its own members. In late September 1980, Led Zeppelin began rehearsing for their next European tour. After a day and night of drinking at Page's home in Windsor, England, Bonham was put to bed. The next day, on September 25, Jones and a tour manager found Bonham dead. He had choked on his own vomit. He was 32 years old and left behind his wife, Pat, and two children, Zoe and Jason. The death was ruled an accident.

The tour was canceled, and the remaining trio was left in shock to process the loss of

Bonham's death meant the end of Led Zeppelin as a band.

their friend and bandmate. Discussions of finding a replacement drummer were short lived and half hearted. "It wouldn't have been Led Zeppelin," said Jones.[1] Without Bonham, there was no future for the band.

On December 4, 1980, Led Zeppelin issued a statement that read, "The loss of our dear friend and the deep sense of harmony felt by ourselves and our manager have led us to decide that we could not continue as we were."[2] After 12 exhilarating, exhausting, chaotic years together, Led Zeppelin would never exist again, and the band members were left to find their own paths forward.

A Life Cut Short

When John Bonham died at age 32, he was remembered as a rock legend and the propelling force behind Led Zeppelin. Bonham's complex beats could shift from thunderous to jazzy, and his commanding solos made it sound as though multiple drummers were playing at once. Known to break two or three pairs of drumsticks a night, he used a Ludwig drum kit, adding congas, timpanis, gongs, and other percussion elements. Bonham is consistently ranked as the top rock drummer of all time, leaving fans to wonder what might have been if not for his untimely death.

ZEPPELIN'S SWAN SONG

In the years following the band's breakup, Page, Plant, and Jones took time apart to mourn their friend's death and look to their next career steps as individual artists. For all their experience, they were relatively young. Page was 36, Jones was 34, and Plant was 32 when Bonham died.

But before its members could move on, the band's contract required it to produce more work for Swan Song Records. It would have to be a compilation of previously recorded tracks because the band wouldn't create new material without Bonham. Page led the effort to produce an album that would be a fitting end to the band's and Bonham's legacy. It would also help satisfy the strong fan interest in more Zeppelin music.

> "It was like staggering away from a great explosion with your eardrums ringing. The dream was over and everything had gone."[3]
>
> *– Robert Plant on the breakup of Led Zeppelin*

Page scoured years of tapes, and Plant and Jones assisted by recording new parts as needed. In 1982, Led Zeppelin released the work as their tenth and final album. Called *Coda*, the album included eight songs dating from 1969 to 1978 that had been recorded in places around the world. The hard-hitting "Wearing and Tearing" had been recorded in 1978 at Sweden's Polar Studio as an answer to the growing punk rock movement. "I Can't Quit You Baby," based on a Willie Dixon blues song, was recorded in 1970

The members of the band, including Jimmy Page, began to go their separate ways in the early 1980s.

during the band's sound check at Royal Albert Hall in London. An homage to their late drummer's skills, "Bonzo's Montreux," had been recorded in 1976 in Montreux, Switzerland.

Coda didn't produce long-standing popular tracks as previous albums had, but that wasn't the point. It helped formally conclude the story of Led Zeppelin. According to music journalist Chris Welch, the album "showed their music was always fresh, original, and brilliantly performed."[4] Named for a musical passage that brings a piece to a close, *Coda* marked the end of an unforgettable chapter in rock history.

ON THEIR OWN

The bandmates soon pursued individual music projects. Plant quickly began releasing his own music. In 1982, Plant released his first solo album, called *Pictures at Eleven*, on Swan Song. It reached Number 3 in the United States and Number 2 in Britain. He followed it up with more success on subsequent solo ventures. His 1984 release *The Honeydrippers: Volume One* covered famous songs from the 1950s and featured guitarists Jeff Beck and Jimmy Page on two tracks each.

Jones focused on his family and continued living up to his reputation as a versatile "musical Swiss Army knife" and "musical polymath"—so labeled by *Rolling Stone* and *Slate*, respectively.[5] He collaborated with a number of artists, including Heart, R.E.M., Brian Eno, and Paul McCartney, in capacities ranging from musician to producer. In 1999, he released his first solo album, *Zooma*.

Leaving "Stairway" Behind

Although "Stairway to Heaven" is one of Led Zeppelin's signature songs, in the decades since the band broke up, Plant hasn't wanted to perform it. He had to be convinced to sing the track at Led Zeppelin's 1988 reunion and has since performed it only a handful of times. Speaking to biographer Mick Wall, Plant explained that he wrote the song's lyrics at another time in his life, and he would prefer to leave the song in the past. "I was a kid, you know?" he said.[6]

Page eventually got out his Les Paul guitar again. In 1984 he and Bad Company vocalist Paul Rodgers formed the band the Firm, which included drummer Chris Slade and bassist Tony Franklin. Its first album produced the hit single "Radioactive." The band split up in 1986. In the midst of various collaboration projects, Page released his first solo album, *Outrider*, in 1988, which featured Plant on one track.

TOGETHER AGAIN

In 1985, the three surviving members of Led Zeppelin reunited at the star-studded Live Aid benefit concert at JFK Stadium in Philadelphia, Pennsylvania. Filling in on drums were Phil

Collins, a successful solo musician formerly of the band Genesis, and Tony Thompson, a session drummer and member of the supergroup the Power Station. The reunion was highly anticipated, as the members of Led Zeppelin had not played together since Bonham's death. Unfortunately, the performance was roundly seen as a misfire, with Plant labeling it "horrendous."[7] Soon after Live Aid, Plant organized a secret practice session with Page, Jones, and Thompson. The group, however, didn't have the same chemistry as in the past, and the idea of playing together again quickly fizzled.

Live Aid

Nothing seemed to go quite right for Led Zeppelin as it made its less-than-triumphant reunion at Live Aid in 1985. The band had limited rehearsal time, Plant's voice was hoarse, Page was given an out-of-tune guitar, and equipment malfunctioned. Most of the 100,000 fans in the crowd—and the nearly two billion watching on television—were too excited about the reunion to notice the glitches, but Zeppelin members were unhappy with the performance and allegedly refused to allow footage of it to appear on the concert DVD.[8]

In 1988, the three bandmates reunited at Madison Square Garden for the fortieth anniversary of Atlantic Records. They performed a five-song set to close out a nearly 13-hour show featuring famous musical acts from the record label's history, from Roberta Flack to the Blues Brothers.

Fans were excited for Zeppelin's reunion at Live Aid, but the band was not satisfied with the results.

> "When you're in a group, you're trying to bring out the best of each member, in that moment. We managed to bring something good out of each other."[9]
>
> *– Jimmy Page, 2012*

Led Zeppelin appeared with Bonham's son, Jason, in his father's place at drums. Still, the bandmates saw the set as an overall disappointment.

Throughout the 1990s, Page led efforts to remaster tracks from Led Zeppelin's catalog, including the previously unreleased "Traveling Riverside Blues" by American blues legend Robert Johnson. Plant and Page teamed up for various performances and eventually began touring together, though not as Led Zeppelin. They released two albums together, though they did not include Jones. Whether it was because of ill will or simply creative differences, the perceived snub sparked questions from fans and the media. With their song "Most High," Plant and Page won their first Grammy in 1998 for Best Hard Rock Performance. In 1995, Led Zeppelin, including Bonham posthumously, was inducted into the Rock & Roll Hall of Fame. "Thank you, my friends, for finally remembering my phone number," remarked Jones during the acceptance speech.[10] The induction featured Led Zeppelin performing with Jason Bonham on drums, along with singer Neil Young and Aerosmith front man Steven Tyler.

UnLedded and Uninvited

In 1994, Plant and Page appeared on MTV's acoustic concert show *Unplugged* in a special performance billed as *UnLedded*. Noticeably absent was Jones, whom the bandmates did not invite. The album resulting from the project, *No Quarter: Jimmy Page and Robert Plant UnLedded*, was salt in the wound for Jones, who cowrote and played a keyboard solo on the song "No Quarter."

CHAPTER NINE

A Long Time Since I Rock and Rolled

Since Led Zeppelin's breakup, rumors have continued regarding a full-scale reunion, with several reports of Led Zeppelin members being on board for such an idea at various times. Reunion performances and releases of compilations of new and live albums have fueled speculations. In 2003, their live album *How the West Was Won*, which featured recordings from 1972 performances in California, hit Number 1.

On December 10, 2007, Led Zeppelin reunited at London's O2 Arena in a tribute to the founder of Atlantic Records, Ahmet Ertegun. The much-anticipated performance marked the first time the trio

Led Zeppelin's 2007 performance at O2 Arena was the band's most successful reunion yet.

had played a full concert together in nearly 30 years. Jason Bonham again took over drumming duties. A reported 20 million people applied to reserve the fewer than 20,000 available tickets through an online lottery system.[1] After Zeppelin's disappointing reunions in 1985 and 1988, this performance was a triumph, with the group reminding audiences why it had been known as the biggest band on Earth.

After the successful concert, Page and Jones began seeking a vocalist when Plant was uninterested in pursuing a reunion project. They tried out singers Steven Tyler of Aerosmith and Myles Kennedy of Slash before killing the idea. "There are absolutely no plans for Led Zeppelin to continue," said Page's manager, Peter Mensch.

Managing Zeppelin

Led Zeppelin manager Peter Grant is credited with revolutionizing the music business and improving conditions and pay for music artists. After working as a tour manager for Chuck Berry, Little Richard, and others, Grant managed the Yardbirds before continuing his close partnership with Page when Led Zeppelin formed. Grant advocated for Led Zeppelin's large signing fee and artistic control through Atlantic Records. He was also the brains behind the band's hugely successful first American tour. Concert promoters at the time typically received a large cut of a show's earnings. However, Grant negotiated Zeppelin's concert contracts so that the band received a majority of the proceeds. He died in 1995 at age 60.

"Zero. Frankly, I wish everybody would stop talking about it."[2]

The O2 performance was released in 2012 as a film called *Celebration Day*, with the resulting album winning a Grammy for Best Rock Album. It was Led Zeppelin's first and only Grammy win. Also in 2012, Led Zeppelin received Kennedy Center Honors, presented by President Barack Obama. The awards are given each year to performing artists for their lifetime contributions to American culture. The ceremony included a tribute to the band by Heart vocalist Ann Wilson and guitarist Nancy Wilson, along with drummer Jason Bonham, backed by a band, horn and string sections, and choir in a powerhouse version of "Stairway to Heaven." As they watched in the audience, the three surviving band members were visibly moved by the performance.

Jason Bonham

Born in 1966, John Bonham's son Jason was a talented drummer by age five. He can be seen drumming on a small kit in the Led Zeppelin concert film *The Song Remains the Same*. In addition to releasing music with bands of his own, he since has played with Foreigner, Paul Rodgers of Bad Company, David Gilmour of Pink Floyd, and of course Led Zeppelin. The surviving members of Led Zeppelin played at Jason's wedding in 1990. Jason uses his father's Led Zeppelin symbol of three interlocking circles on his website and his line of drumsticks.

LIFE AFTER ZEPPELIN

Throughout the 2000s, Page continued to oversee Led Zeppelin's legacy, including the remastering process of all of the band's studio albums, which were released to massive success between 2014 and 2015 as CDs, downloads, and vinyl. Page also oversaw releases of expanded sets and previously unreleased tracks. In 2005, Queen Elizabeth named Page an Officer of the British Empire (OBE), a high British honor, for his charity work in Brazil. Page had worked with a British charity to set up a facility that provided more than 300 children with food, clothing, medicine, and other support. In a 2012 interview, he reported being sober for many years.

In 2009, Plant's collaboration with bluegrass singer Alison Krauss earned the duo five Grammys, including Album of the Year for *Raising Sand* and Record of the Year for the track "Please Read the Letter." Since Led Zeppelin's breakup, Plant has

Lifetime Award

Despite the band's tremendous success, Led Zeppelin was largely ignored for industry awards during its time as an active band. In 2005, Led Zeppelin received a Grammy Lifetime Achievement Award. Page and Jones accepted the award, while Plant sent a video message. Bonham's children were also on hand to accept the award in his place. "The legend lives on," said Bonham's daughter, Zoe.[3]

Plant's work with Krauss achieved both critical and commercial success.

released more than ten studio albums. In 2012, he formed the rock band Sensational Space Shifters. Although he was adamant that Led Zeppelin was part of the past, his various bands play versions of Zeppelin classics, and as of 2020 his website bore his famous Zeppelin symbol of an encircled feather. In 2009, he was honored as a Commander of the British Empire (CBE).

Jones continued his prolific work with artists such as bluegrass acts Nickel Creek and Seasick Steve and released experimental and improvisational music. He formed a supergroup called Them

Crooked Vultures, active from 2009 to 2010, that included Dave Grohl of the Foo Fighters and Josh Homme of Queens of the Stone Age. The group's song "New Fang" won a 2010 Grammy for Best Hard Rock Performance. In 2018, Jones released more information about the opera he had been working on for several years. Called *The Ghost Sonata*, it was based on a Swedish play.

Led Zeppelin also continued to deal with copyright issues. In 2014, a representative of the band Spirit filed a lawsuit against the band claiming the intro to "Stairway to Heaven" was plagiarized from Spirit's 1968 instrumental song "Taurus," which Led Zeppelin denied. Two years later, the three surviving members of Led Zeppelin were called to testify in a trial on the subject. Led Zeppelin won the lawsuit, but an appeal followed. A retrial took place in September 2019. A ruling was expected in 2020. The case stirred up conversations about how to set legal standards on music. Copyright experts continued watching the

> "I'd say it was a rip-off. And the guys made millions of bucks on it and never said, 'Thank you,' never said, 'Can we pay you some money for it?' It's kind of a sore point with me."[4]
>
> *– Randy Wolfe of Spirit, on "Stairway to Heaven," 1996*

case closely for possible long-term effects on the music industry.

LEGENDS OF ROCK

In 2018, Led Zeppelin marked 50 years since their formation. Soon after, the trio confirmed the first official documentary film about Led Zeppelin was underway, featuring new interviews with the surviving members and archival footage of Bonham. For many fans, the film would be a welcome insight into the best-selling band whose legend continues to loom larger than life decades after their first record hit turntables. That rock star legend has only grown in proportion, with wild true stories combining with rumor and speculation.

Meanwhile, the revolutionary force of Led Zeppelin has come into sharper focus as music continues to evolve. Not content to play rock or blues as they were known, Zeppelin developed new sounds and textures, bringing in elements of folk, psychedelia, classical, country, funk, jazz, soul, reggae, world music, and what would later be considered the precursors to punk and progressive rock.

> "A Led Zeppelin song could captivate and bore within the space of a few minutes. A big part of their genius was that they thought it was OK to do both."[5]
>
> – *Ann Powers,* Los Angeles Times

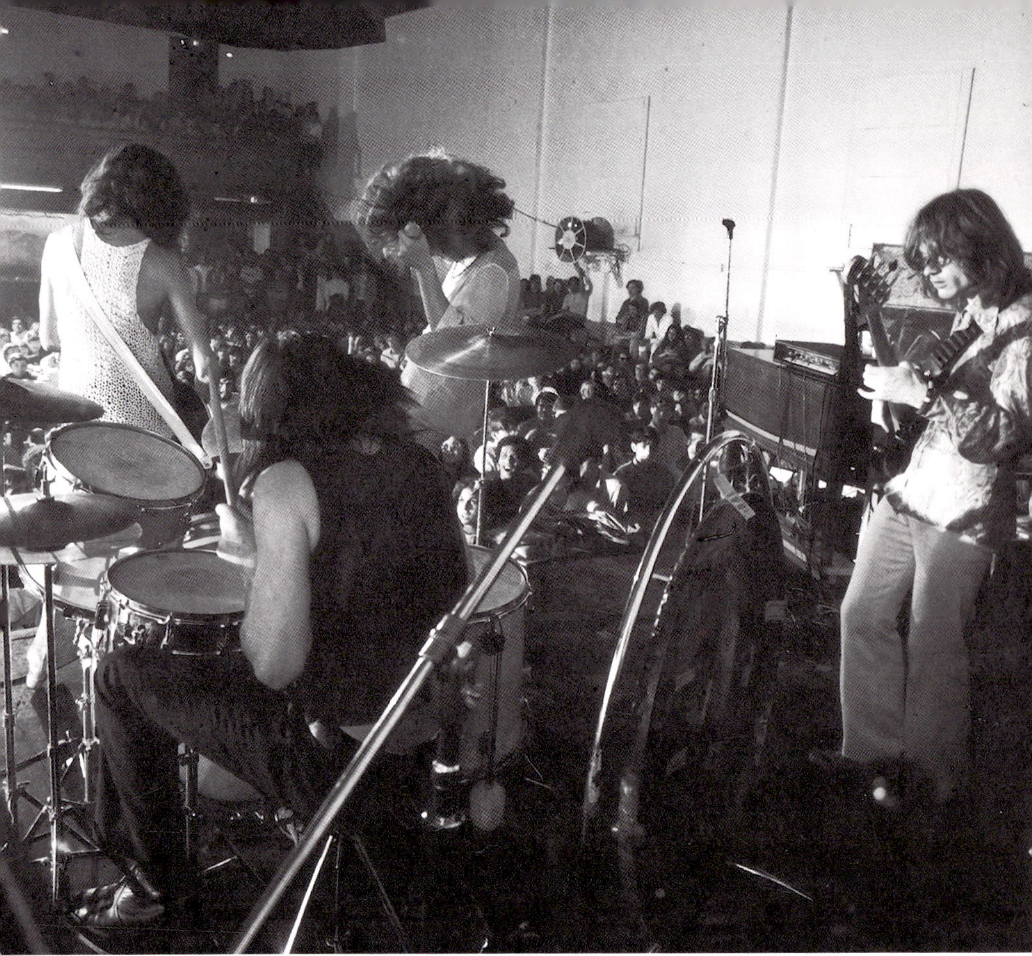

Though Led Zeppelin has been broken up for more than 40 years, their musical and cultural legacy will continue for generations to come.

According to Jack Hamilton of *Slate*, "Their influence, for better and worse, over all that's come since is singular. Punk in the 1970s was a rejection of their pompous pretentiousness, metal in the 1980s an affirmation of their excesses, grunge in the 1990s a reclamation of punk that often sounded a lot like Led Zeppelin."[6]

From their innovative use of sound techniques to their explosive, large-scale live performances,

Led Zeppelin has continued to inspire artists representing a variety of genres, including the Ramones, the Beastie Boys, Tori Amos, Lenny Kravitz, the Foo Fighters, and the White Stripes. Additionally, with manager Peter Grant's negotiating skills and forward thinking, Led Zeppelin set new precedents for artistic control and earnings. Their music has stood the test of time, welcoming new fans of all generations even as present-day listeners question the band's excessive and often damaging rock and roll lifestyle.

When Bonham, Jones, Page, and Plant played together for the first time in 1968, they knew they had something special—and audiences knew it too. Their chemistry was potent, their music raw, their performances thrilling, their musical talents undeniable. With their fearless intensity and creative energy, Led Zeppelin cemented their place in music history as one of the greatest rock bands of all time.

> "It's the music that keeps the band buoyant, rather than the myth. When the myth fades, the music will still be there."[7]
>
> *– Jimmy Page, 2012*

TIMELINE

1968

Jimmy Page recruits John Paul Jones, Robert Plant, and John Bonham for his new band. In August, the four members rehearse for the first time together in London. In September, the group plays its first gig as the New Yardbirds in Denmark. They soon change their name to Led Zeppelin.

1969

In January, Led Zeppelin releases their self-titled debut album. In October, Led Zeppelin releases *Led Zeppelin II*.

1970

In October, Led Zeppelin releases *Led Zeppelin III*.

1971

In November, Led Zeppelin releases their untitled fourth album, known as *Led Zeppelin IV* or "Four Symbols."

1973

In March, Led Zeppelin releases the *Houses of the Holy* album.

1974

In May, Led Zeppelin starts the Swan Song record label under Atlantic Records.

1975

In February, Led Zeppelin releases the *Physical Graffiti* album. In August, Plant and his family are involved in a serious car accident.

1976

In April, Led Zeppelin releases the *Presence* album.

1977

In July, Plant's son, Karac, dies. The band takes a break as it regroups.

1979

In August, Led Zeppelin releases the album *In Through the Out Door*.

1980

On September 25, Bonham is found dead at Page's home. Led Zeppelin breaks up.

1982

Led Zeppelin releases the album *Coda*, a compilation of previously recorded tracks.

1985

The surviving members of Led Zeppelin reunite at Live Aid.

1988

The surviving members of Led Zeppelin reunite at Madison Square Garden.

1995

Led Zeppelin is inducted into the Rock & Roll Hall of Fame.

2007

In December, the surviving members of Led Zeppelin reunite for a full concert at London's O2 Arena.

2012

Celebration Day, the film from the O2 performance, is released. The soundtrack album wins Led Zeppelin their first Grammy.

ESSENTIAL FACTS

Led Zeppelin Band Members

- **John Bonham** was the band's drummer. He died in 1980.
- **John Paul Jones** played bass and keyboards in the band.
- **Jimmy Page** played guitar in the band.
- **Robert Plant** was the band's lead singer.

Led Zeppelin Studio Albums

- *Led Zeppelin* (1969)
- *Led Zeppelin II* (1969)
- *Led Zeppelin III* (1970)
- *Untitled* [Led Zeppelin IV] (1971)
- *Houses of the Holy* (1973)
- *Physical Graffiti* (1975)
- *Presence* (1976)
- *In Through the Out Door* (1979)

Career Highlights

Led Zeppelin garnered tremendous attendance numbers at their live shows, overtaking the Beatles for the highest attendance at a single show, breaking that record in 1973. Their legacy culminated with their induction into the Rock & Roll Hall of Fame in 1995. In 2012, Led Zeppelin won their first Grammy award as a band for Best Rock Album, *Celebration Day*. Their albums continue to be popular decades after their initial releases, with an estimated 300 million albums sold to date and several included on present-day lists of best rock albums of all time.

Conflicts

Despite a fervent fan base, Led Zeppelin received many negative reviews by music critics throughout their active years, most infamously in *Rolling Stone*. As the group's star status skyrocketed, it experienced rising tensions, and some members took part in increasingly reckless behavior through drugs and alcohol. Events that contributed to the band's crumbling foundation included a 1975 car accident involving Robert Plant and his family, followed two years later by the death of Plant's son, Karac. In 1980, John Bonham's alcohol-related death marked the band's official breakup.

Quote

"When you're in a group, you're trying to bring out the best of each member, in that moment. We managed to bring something good out of each other."

– Jimmy Page, 2012

GLOSSARY

a cappella
Without instruments.

acoustic
Without electrical amplification.

astrology
The study of the supposed influence of planets and stars on human activities.

B side
The other side of a record; the "A side" generally had the promoted single.

counterculture
A culture of values that go against those of established society, popularized in the 1960s.

cover
A song that was previously recorded by someone else.

debut
The first appearance, often of an album or publication, made by a musician or group.

double album
An extra-long album released on two vinyl records rather than the usual one.

front man
The leader in a band, usually the singer.

improvisational
Created without preparation.

misogynistic
Having hatred of or contempt for women.

mythology
Traditional stories or legends.

occultist
A person who believes in or practices magic and the supernatural.

panned
Sharply criticized.

parodied
Imitated or exaggerated for comic effect.

plagiarism
The act of copying and claiming another person's words or ideas as your own.

polymath
A person who has a wide range of knowledge.

posthumously
Happening after someone's death.

psychedelia
The set of people, places, things, and ideas associated with the use of psychedelic drugs.

samba
Brazilian dance music.

session musician
A musician hired to work in a recording session or performance rather than as a permanent member of a band.

tempo
The speed of a piece of music.

ADDITIONAL RESOURCES

Selected Bibliography

Gilmore, Mikal. "The Long Shadow of Led Zeppelin," *Rolling Stone*, 10 Aug. 2006, rollingstone.com. Accessed 10 Jan. 2020.

Wall, Mick. *When Giants Walked the Earth: A Biography of Led Zeppelin*. St. Martin's Griffin, 2019.

Welch, Chris. *Led Zeppelin: The Ultimate Collection*. Carlton Books, 2015.

Further Readings

Buck, Kevin. *A Concise History of Rock 'n' Roll*. Year of the Book, 2018.

Kortemeier, Todd. *Pink Floyd*. Abdo, 2022.

Robertson, Robbie. *Legends, Icons & Rebels: Music that Changed the World*. Tundra, 2013.

Online Resources

To learn more about Led Zeppelin, please visit **abdobooklinks.com** or scan this QR code. These links are routinely monitored and updated to provide the most current information available.

More Information

For more information on this subject, contact or visit the following organizations:

Atlantic Records
1633 Broadway
New York, NY 10019
212-707-2000
atlanticrecords.com

Led Zeppelin signed with Atlantic Records in 1968.

Rock & Roll Hall of Fame
1100 Rock and Roll Blvd.
Cleveland, OH 44114
216-781-7625
rockhall.com

Led Zeppelin was inducted into the Rock & Roll Hall of Fame in 1995.

SOURCE NOTES

CHAPTER 1. ROCKING THE GARDEN

1. "Led Zeppelin – Stairway to Heaven – Madison Square Garden, New York City." *YouTube*, uploaded by Syd Le Corbusier, 10 Aug. 2011, youtube.com. Accessed 17 Aug. 2019.
2. "July 29, 1973." *Led Zeppelin*, n.d., ledzeppelin.com. Accessed 17 Aug. 2019.
3. "NY 7-29-73: Jimmy Page Interview." *Led Zeppelin*, n.d., ledzeppelin.com. Accessed 21 Jan. 2020.
4. Mick Wall. *When Giants Walked the Earth: A Biography of Led Zeppelin*. St. Martin's Press, 2009. 132.
5. Keith Caulfield. "Led Zeppelin Heading Back to the Top 10, Again." *Billboard*, 6 Aug. 2015, billboard.com. Accessed 9 Aug. 2019.

CHAPTER 2. ON THE WINGS OF YARDBIRDS

1. Mick Wall. *When Giants Walked the Earth: A Biography of Led Zeppelin.* St. Martin's Press, 2009. 73.
2. Wall, *When Giants Walked the Earth*, 45–46.
3. Chris Welch. *Led Zeppelin: The Ultimate Collection*. Carlton Books, 2015. 13.
4. "September 7, 1968." *Led Zeppelin*, n.d., ledzeppelin.com. Accessed 17 Aug. 2019.
5. "September 7, 1968."
6. Andy Greene. "The 10 Wildest Led Zeppelin Legends, Fact-Checked." *Rolling Stone*, 16 Oct. 2019, rollingstone.com. Accessed 21 Jan. 2020.
7. Welch, *Led Zeppelin*, 13.

CHAPTER 3. LEAD BALLOON RISING

1. Chris Welch. "Obituary: Peter Grant." *Independent*, 24 Nov. 1995, independent.co.uk. Accessed 21 Jan. 2020.
2. Lisa Robinson. "Stairway to Excess." *Vanity Fair*, 18 Feb. 2014, vanityfair.com. Accessed 9 Mar. 2020.
3. Mick Wall. *When Giants Walked the Earth: A Biography of Led Zeppelin.* St. Martin's Press, 2009. 101.
4. Wall, *When Giants Walked the Earth*, 81.
5. Brielle Schiavone. "Remembering the Boston Show that Prophesized the Rise of Led Zeppelin." *Consequence of Sound*, 7 Feb. 2019, consequenceofsound.net. Accessed 17 Sept. 2019.
6. John Mendelsohn. "Led Zeppelin I." *Rolling Stone*, 15 Mar. 1969, rollingstone.com. Accessed 14 Feb. 2020.
7. Greg Kot. "Led Zeppelin." *Rolling Stone*, 20 Aug. 2001, rollingstone.com. Accessed 21 Jan. 2020.

CHAPTER 4. THE TIME IS NOW

1. Matt Wardlaw. "Cameron Crowe Recalls Battle for Led Zeppelin Cover Story." *Ultimate Classic Guitar*, 28 Dec. 2011, ultimateclassicrock.com. Accessed 14 Dec. 2019.

2. Leslie Richin. "Today in 1968 Led Zeppelin Kicked Off First US Tour." *Billboard*, 26 Dec. 2014, billboard.com. Accessed 21 Dec. 2019.

3. Patrick Doyle. "How 'Led Zeppelin II' Was Born." *Rolling Stone*, 22 Oct. 2019, rollingstone.com. Accessed 21 Dec. 2019.

4. Doyle, "How 'Led Zeppelin II' Was Born."

5. "500 Greatest Albums of All Time." *Rolling Stone*, 31 May 2012, rollingstone.com. Accessed 14 Dec. 2019.

6. Marc Myers. "How One of Led Zeppelin's Greatest Hits Was Made." *Business Insider*, 2 Dec. 2016, businessinsider.com. Accessed 14 Feb. 2020.

7. Myers, "How One of Led Zeppelin's Greatest Hits Was Made."

8. Cameron Crowe. "Led Zeppelin: The Song Remains the Same Reissue (2007)." *The Uncool*, Aug. 2007, theuncool.com. Accessed 2 Oct. 2019.

9. Jordan Runtagh. "Songs on Trial: 12 Landmark Music Copyright Cases." *Rolling Stone*, 8 June 2016, rollingstone.com. Accessed 14 Dec. 2019.

10. Mick Wall. *When Giants Walked the Earth: A Biography of Led Zeppelin*. St. Martin's Press, 2009. 199.

11. Chris Welch. *Led Zeppelin: The Ultimate Collection*. Carlton Books, 2015. 32.

CHAPTER 5. CLIMBING TO NEW HEIGHTS

1. "July 5, 1971." *Led Zeppelin*, n.d., ledzeppelin.com. Accessed 17 Aug. 2019.

2. "March 5, 1971." *Led Zeppelin*, n.d., ledzeppelin.com. Accessed 17 Aug. 2019.

3. Jordan Runtagh. "Led Zeppelin's 'Houses of the Holy': 10 Things You Didn't Know." *Rolling Stone*, 28 Mar. 2018, rollingstone.com. Accessed 20 Dec. 2019.

4. "May 4, 1973." *Led Zeppelin*, n.d., ledzeppelin.com. Accessed 15 Dec. 2019.

5. "July 29, 1973." *Led Zeppelin*, n.d., ledzeppelin.com. Accessed 17 Aug. 2019.

6. Chris Welch. *Led Zeppelin: The Ultimate Collection*. Carlton Books, 2015. 21.

7. "July 29, 1973."

8. "July 29, 1973."

9. Erik Davis. "What Exactly Lurks within the Backwards Grooves of 'Stairway to Heaven?'" *Salon*, 24 June 2017, salon.com. Accessed 24 Sept. 2019.

SOURCE NOTES CONTINUED

10. Cameron Crowe. "Led Zeppelin: The Song Remains the Same Reissue (2007)." *The Uncool*, Aug. 2007, theuncool.com. Accessed 2 Oct. 2019.

11. Welch, *Led Zeppelin*, 43.

CHAPTER 6. ON TOP OF THE WORLD

1. Mick Wall. "How Presence Pulled Led Zeppelin Back from the Brink of Crisis." *Louder*, 14 July 2017, loudersound.com. Accessed 4 Oct. 2019.

2. Mick Wall. *When Giants Walked the Earth: A Biography of Led Zeppelin*. St. Martin's Press, 2009. 322.

3. Cameron Crowe. "The Durable Led Zeppelin." *Rolling Stone*, 13 Mar. 1975, rollingstone.com. Accessed 20 Sept. 2019.

4. Crowe, "The Durable Led Zeppelin."

5. Chris Welch. *Led Zeppelin: The Ultimate Collection*. Carlton Books, 2015. 72.

6. Cameron Crowe. "Led Zeppelin Conquers the States." *Rolling Stone*, 22 May 1975, rollingstone.com. Accessed 20 Sept. 2019.

CHAPTER 7. CRASHING DOWN

1. Mikal Gilmore. "The Long Shadow of Led Zeppelin." *Rolling Stone*, 10 Aug. 2006, rollingstone.com. Accessed 26 Sept. 2019.

2. "July 24, 1977." *Led Zeppelin*, n.d., ledzeppelin.com. Accessed 28 Sept. 2019.

3. William Langley. "Song Remains the Same." *Telegraph*, 9 Dec. 2007, telegraph.co.uk. Accessed 21 Dec. 2019.

4. Lisa Robinson. "Stairway to Excess." *Vanity Fair*, 18 Feb. 2014, vanityfair.com. Accessed 26 Sept. 2019.

5. Corbin Reiff. "Listen to this Eddie: Inside the Tour that Grounded Led Zeppelin with Drugs, Violence, and Tragedy." *Uproxx*, 22 June 2017, uproxx.com. Accessed 28 Sept. 2019.

6. Gilmore, "The Long Shadow of Led Zeppelin."

7. Mick Wall. *When Giants Walked the Earth: A Biography of Led Zeppelin*. St. Martin's Press, 2009. 375.

8. Gilmore, "The Long Shadow of Led Zeppelin."

9. Robinson, "Stairway to Excess."

10. "August 4, 1979." *Led Zeppelin*, n.d., ledzeppelin.com. Accessed 28 Sept. 2019.

CHAPTER 8. END OF A DREAM

1. Chris Welch. *Led Zeppelin: The Ultimate Collection*. Carlton Books, 2015. 82.

2. Richard Harrington. "Led Zeppelin's Stairway to Concert Heaven." *Washington Post*, 25 May 2003, washingtonpost.com. Accessed 21 Jan. 2020.

3. Welch, *Led Zeppelin*, 83.

4. Welch, *Led Zeppelin*, 85.

5. Jack Hamilton. "Good Times Bad Times." *Slate*, 18 June 2014, slate.com. Accessed 14 Sept. 2019.

6. Mick Wall. *When Giants Walked the Earth: A Biography of Led Zeppelin*. St. Martin's Press, 2009. 432.

7. Andy Greene. "Flashback: Led Zeppelin Reunite (Badly) at Live Aid." *Rolling Stone*, 11 Mar. 2014, rollingstone.com. Accessed 21 Jan. 2020.

8. David Morton. "Live Aid, 1985: Thirty-two Years Ago Today, We Were Rocking All Over the World." *Chronicle*, 13 July 2017, chroniclelive.co.uk. Accessed 22 Dec. 2019.

9. David Fricke. "Jimmy Page: The Rolling Stone Interview." *Rolling Stone*, 6 Dec. 2012, rollingstone.com. Accessed 21 Dec. 2019.

10. "John Paul Jones Made Things Awkward During His Acceptance Speech at the Rock & Roll Hall of Fame." *Society of Rock*, n.d., societyofrock.com. Accessed 21 Jan. 2020.

CHAPTER 9. A LONG TIME SINCE I ROCK AND ROLLED

1. Natalie Paris. "20 Million Led Zeppelin Fans Rush for Tickets." *Telegraph*, 13 Sept. 2007, telegraph.co.uk. Accessed 29 Sept. 2019.

2. Martin Kielty. "10 More Years Gone: Why the 2007 Reunion was Led Zeppelin's Last Stand." *Ultimate Classic Rock*, 8 Dec. 2017, ultimateclassicrock.com. Accessed 28 Sept. 2019.

3. "Grammy Lifetime Achievement Award." *Led Zeppelin*, n.d., ledzeppelin.com. Accessed 1 Oct. 2019.

4. Caitlin Gibson. "Robert Plant Testifies He Can't Read Music or Remember The 60s. Verdict: Still a Rockstar." *Washington Post*, 22 June 2016, washingtonpost.com. Accessed 14 Sept. 2016.

5. Ann Powers. "From Zep Hater to a Whole Lotta Love." *Los Angeles Times*, 2 Dec 2007, latimes.com. Accessed 5 Oct. 2019.

6. Jack Hamilton. "Good Times Bad Times." *Slate*, 18 June 2014, slate.com. Accessed 14 Sept. 2019.

7. David Fricke. "Jimmy Page: The Rolling Stone Interview." *Rolling Stone*, 6 Dec. 2012, rollingstone.com. Accessed 21 Dec. 2019.

INDEX

ABOUT THE AUTHOR

Laura K. Murray

Laura K. Murray is the Minnesota-based author of more than 70 books on subjects ranging from music and pop culture to history and science. Her favorite part of writing this book was listening to Led Zeppelin's albums as their story unfolded.